ANIMALS ON THE EDGE

The Mystery of WHALE STRANDINGS

A Cause and Effect Investigation

by Jody Sullivan Rake

Consultant:
Deborah Nuzzolo
Manager, Education and Conservation
SeaWorld, San Diego

CAPSTONE PRESS
a capstone imprint

Fact Finders are published by Capstone Press,
151 Good Counsel Drive, P.O. Box 669, Mankato, Minnesota 56002.
www.capstonepub.com

032010
005740CGF10

 Books published by Capstone Press are manufactured with paper
containing at least 10 percent post-consumer waste.

Library of Congress Cataloging-in-Publication Data
Rake, Jody Sullivan.
  The mystery of whale strandings : a cause and effect investigation / by Jody Sullivan Rake.
     p. cm. — (Fact finders. Animals on the edge)
  Summary: "Describes the cause and effect of whale strandings"—Provided by publisher.
  ISBN 978-1-4296-4531-7 (library binding)
  1. Whales--Stranding—Juvenile literature. I. Title. II. Series.

QL737.C4R23 2011
599.5—dc22   2010008561

Editorial Credits
Marissa Bolte, editor; Ashlee Suker, designer; Kelly Garvin, media researcher;
     Eric Manske, production specialist

Photo Credits
Corbis/Ho/Reuters, 4; Natalie Fobes, 16; Reuters, 14; Theo Allofs, 13
Getty Images/AFP, cover; Brandon Cole, 21; Greg Wood, 25; Paul Nicklen, 23;
     Sandra Teddy, 7; Sue Flood, 20
Mary Evans Picture Library, 5
Seapics/Bryan & Cherry Alexander, 10; Christopher Swann, 22; Doug Perrine, 12, 26;
     Masa Ushioda, 11; Richard Herrmann, 18; Robert L. Pitman, 6; Roland Seitre, 8
Shutterstock/Ron Rutgers, design element (water ripples); S. Hanusch, 17

TABLE OF CONTENTS

CHAPTER 1

Stranded!

In March 2009, a familiar sight was seen off the coast of Australia. More than 190 pilot whales and seven dolphins lay stranded on Tasmania's King Island. Rescuers tried to return the animals to sea. Still, only 54 whales and five dolphins were saved.

Year after year, whale strandings make headlines. But strandings have been baffling scientists for centuries. They have **theories** about what could be causing the strandings, but no solid answers.

More than 80 percent of whale strandings in Australia happen on the island of Tasmania.

In the past, beached whales were seen as a source of food. Today deciding what to do with the whales is a complex problem.

The earliest recorded whale strandings date back to 2300 BC. Official records on strandings have been kept since 1840. Many people believe that strandings have increased. They wonder if it's because of growing human populations. Others think that the strandings haven't increased, but the reports have.

A stranded whale or dolphin is usually one that is stuck on shore. But it could also be a whale that swam into a bay or lagoon and can't find its way back to the open sea.

theory—an idea that explains something that is unknown

Because of their size, rescuing large whales, like sperm whales, is difficult.

Some whale species are known to strand more than others. Nearly 90 percent of all strandings involve only five whale **species** and one dolphin species. The whale species include the pilot, sperm, false killer, pygmy sperm, and Gray's beaked. The common dolphin is also known to strand.

Experts identify two types of strandings—single and mass. Single strandings involve an individual whale of any species. They happen at just about any place and time. Single strandings almost always occur when an animal is ill, injured, or weak.

species—a group of animals with similar features

A mass stranding is when two or more adult whales of the same species come ashore. The whales strand at about the same time and place. Mass strandings are not as easily understood as single strandings. Often a mass stranding involves a group of healthy animals. This fact adds to the mystery of why strandings happen. But there are some patterns in mass strandings.

More than 90 percent of all mass strandings involve pilot whales or false killer whales.

Pilot whales live in the open ocean. They can easily become confused in unfamiliar, shallow water.

Scientists have found that species that live in deep water commonly strand. Shallow beaches and rough shorelines can confuse whales used to the open sea.

Pilot whales are one of the most common whale species that mass strand. The largest mass stranding ever recorded occurred in 1918. More than 1,000 pilot whales came ashore in New Zealand.

False killer whales also mass strand. The largest mass stranding of these whales happened in 1946. People found 835 whales washed up on the beach of Mar del Plata, Argentina.

Whale Strandings, 2000–Present

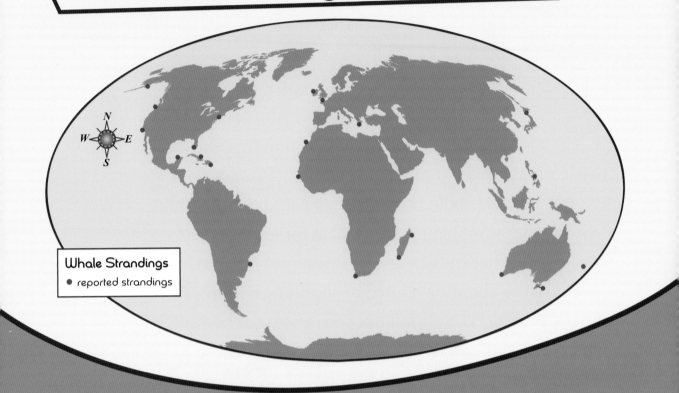

Whale Strandings
• reported strandings

Follow the Leader

Mass strandings always involve toothed whales. Toothed whales live in highly social groups called pods. Because **baleen** whales do not live in groups, they do not mass strand. One or two dominant whales control the rest of the pod. If the leader does something, the pod will follow—even if the leader is injured or confused. Nothing can stop a pod of whales from following their leader. They will follow, even to their doom. This is just one theory as to why whales mass strand.

WHAT CAUSES WHALES TO STRAND?

baleen—plates in a whale's mouth that help it eat

CHAPTER 2
Ailing Whales

The more scientists study whale strandings, the more they learn about what might cause them. Whales with serious physical problems are likely to strand. Something is wrong that is making it impossible for them to live a normal life. What could some of those problems be?

Injury is a common source of strandings. Injuries cause loss of blood, shock, infection, and weakness. Injuries can come from predators like sharks. These wounds have been seen on a number of occasions. Human activities also threaten whales. Each year more than 300,000 **cetaceans** die after getting tangled in fishing nets.

Nets are not the only threats to whales. Bullet wounds have been seen on the bodies of stranded whales too.

Tail fin injuries make it hard for a whale to swim well enough to catch prey or escape from predators.

Scientists also believe infection plays a role in whale strandings. In 1986, 14 pilot whales beached in Cape Cod, Massachusetts. Scientists found that the whales were suffering from a type of flu virus. In the ocean, whales are exposed to many microscopic invaders. Hundreds of different bacteria and viruses float from one animal to another. **Parasites** such as internal roundworms slowly eat away at whales from the inside.

cetacean—the scientific name for whales, dolphins, and porpoises
parasite—an animal or plant that needs to live on or inside another animal or plant to survive

Toothed whales often hunt in groups.

Starvation also threatens whales. Food is not always easy to find. Hungry whales will chase prey all the way to the shore. But the whales are often unable to find their way back to sea.

Separation is a common threat to whale calves. In 1997 workers at SeaWorld rescued an orphaned gray whale calf near Los Angeles. Without its mother, the calf would have died in less than a day. Without their mothers' milk, protection, and guidance, calves fall victim to predators or end up washed on shore.

Some whale species fall victim to their own fear. When frightened, sperm whales swim off in one direction. If they are headed straight toward shore, they will strand. Smaller whales may be herded into shallow water by larger predators. Killer whales use this technique. They shepherd panicking dolphins and seals toward the shoreline. In the shallow water, the smaller animals are unable to escape.

Killer whales hunt seals, fish, and more than 20 species of cetaceans.

Disruptions in a whale's **echolocation** also cause strandings. Echolocation helps whales find their way in deep ocean water. Whales use echolocation to "see" things around them. Certain diseases and parasites can damage parts of the head used for echolocation. If they are unable to see, they may become confused and crash into rocks or coral reefs. All of these factors help explain stranding behavior, especially single strandings.

Even after being rescued, some whales may be too tired or confused to swim back out to sea.

Whale Echolocation

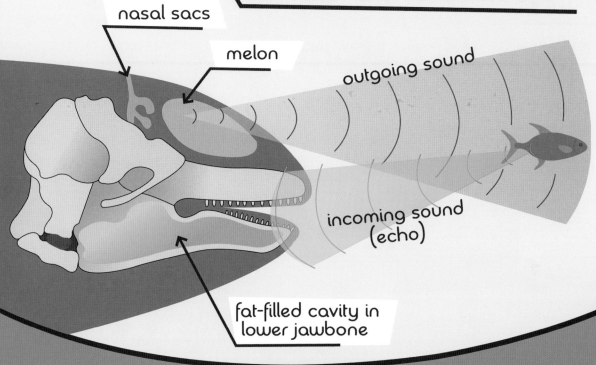

nasal sacs

melon

outgoing sound

incoming sound
(echo)

fat-filled cavity in
lower jawbone

What Is Echolocation?

Toothed whales rely on echolocation to navigate. They can produce high-pitched sound waves in their nasal cavities. The sound waves leave through the whale's melon and travel through the water. The sound waves bounce off nearby objects and echo back to the whale. The whale receives sound waves through its lower jaw. The sound waves are transmitted to the whale's ear and then the brain. These signals give a whale information about objects and obstacles. The whale can figure out the size, shape, and distance of anything in its way.

WHAT CAUSES MASS STRANDINGS OF HEALTHY WHALES?

echolocation—the process of using sounds and echoes to locate objects

CHAPTER 3

Under the Weather

In 1999 and 2000, a record number of gray whales washed up on the Pacific coast between Alaska and Mexico.

Physical conditions are not the only reason whales strand. Environmental conditions, like severe weather and **global warming**, are becoming more of a concern too.

In winter 1998, 97 dolphins died off the coast of Cape Cod, Massachusetts. Scientists believe that severe winter storms may have been the cause. Even though whales are designed for ocean life, they can still be hurt by the weather. Strong waves may thrash animals about. Whales that are hurt or worn out may wash up during a storm.

global warming—the gradual temperature rise of Earth's atmosphere

Recently scientists have become concerned with global warming trends. Even a slight warming in Earth's atmosphere can be harmful to whales. Temperature changes can cause a drop in the amount of prey. These trends may also alter shorelines and make them difficult for whales to navigate.

El Niño

In the Pacific Ocean, El Niño may be to blame for an increase in whale strandings. This event occurs every two to seven years. It is marked by warming of the sea surface and often severe weather. Much of the whales' food supply heads for colder waters. The whales are left to face starvation and storms.

Some stranded whales have shown evidence of inner-ear damage caused by boats.

The ocean is surprisingly full of sounds. Sounds can be both natural and man-made. Sound waves travel more than four times farther under water than in air. Whales have a well-developed sense of hearing. To them, many noises can be both frightening and damaging.

Underwater earthquakes create loud rumblings in the sea. A strong earthquake can cause a sound blast strong enough to scare whales toward shore. The blast could also damage the air sacs that help whales sense vibrations under water. The noise produced by thousands of ships at sea can also throw a pod off course.

Military **sonar** is another concern. Sonar creates pulses of sound under water called pings. The pings can disrupt whales' navigation systems, causing them to swim off-course. Some people fear that the loud pings are also damaging to whales' ears.

In January 2005, 36 whales of varying species stranded in North Carolina. Afterward it was found that sonar testing had taken place in nearby waters. Some believe the two events are connected. But others believe that sonar is only damaging when it is extremely loud and very close. Is sonar dangerous to whales? Much more study is needed to answer that question.

Some scientists believe that whales are sensitive to Earth's magnetic field. They may even navigate by it. Scientists believe that changes in the magnetic field confuse whales. The confused animals then swim off-course and strand. Scientists continue to look for evidence to prove this theory.

sonar—a device that uses sound waves to find underwater objects; sonar stands for sound navigation and ranging

Some whale species spend their entire lives within a few miles of the shore. Living this close to the edge of land has its dangers.

In the Arctic, beluga whales are known to swim into shallow waters to catch prey. Sometimes they stay too long and get stuck on land when the tide goes out. Sometimes they can safely swim away when the high tide returns. Others are not so lucky and die on land.

Arctic whales often feed near the edge of the ice pack in autumn. This time of year, the ocean quickly freezes. Watery passages turn into ice. Whales get trapped as the ice cuts off their only escape. In 1994 whale experts rescued seven killer whales that were trapped by ice in Barnes Lake, Alaska. Other whales end up dying in or on top of the new ice.

Whales use holes in the ice to breathe and rest. If the holes freeze over, the whales won't be able to take fresh breaths of air and will suffocate.

Oil tankers are major threats to whales. Their cargo can be hazardous if it spills. The large ships sometimes strike and kill sleeping or resting whales.

Humans share the coastline with whales. Human activities are another growing concern. Pollution dumped into the ocean ends up in a whale's food supply. Oil that travels around the globe for fuel is also a hazard. If even a little oil spills into the sea, it can be deadly. If the oil gets into the whales' blowholes, they can suffocate and die.

WHAT CAN PEOPLE DO TO HELP WHALES?

CHAPTER 4
Save the Whales

For all living things, death is a natural part of the life cycle. Most whales that strand are close to death for many reasons. No one likes the thought of such magnificent animals hurt and dying. But there are other reasons to be concerned too.

Are whale strandings increasing? Are whale strandings a sign of looming environmental disaster? What affects whales in the ocean now will eventually affect life on land. Is this a warning?

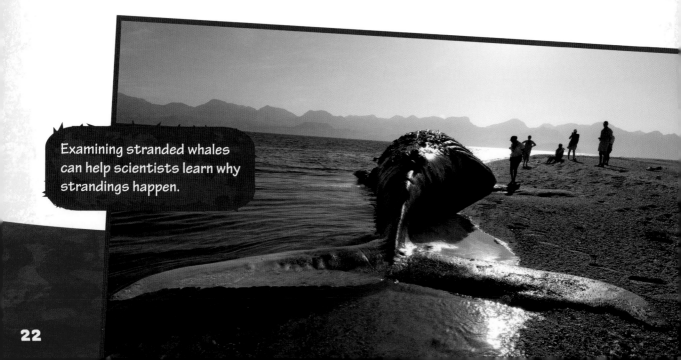

Examining stranded whales can help scientists learn why strandings happen.

Scientists tag live whales to monitor their movements in the ocean.

Are humans doing something to cause this? Scientists have noticed that, as the environment changes, so does the feeding and breeding patterns of whales. By observing these changes, the whales help make people aware of how their choices affect the planet.

When people witness a whale stranding, their first reaction is to return the whales to the sea. But well-meaning, inexperienced people can cause the whales more harm. Whale strandings are best left to the experts who have the knowledge and resources to handle them. Rescuers must consider two very important questions.

First, would returning the whales to the sea be harmful to the population? If the whales are sick, they could infect others.

Second, is it possible? Stranding is very stressful for whales. Without water to cool them, whales overheat quickly. And on land, whales are not supported by water. They are unable to hold up their massive bodies. Eventually their huge bodies will crush their skeletons and organs. These animals are not likely to survive even if they are returned to the water. Some whales may turn right around and strand again. Giant whales, like sperm whales, are nearly impossible to move from the shore.

Rescuers must work quickly. Sometimes rescuers apply a sunscreen called zinc oxide. Whales are kept moist with water and wet towels. Other times rescuers try to return a stranded whale to the ocean.

Rescuers must wait for the tide to come back in before helping stranded whales.

If rescuers are able to refloat a stranded whale, they often use a specially designed whale stretcher. They gently roll the whale onto the stretcher and carry it to deeper water. With the right conditions, a whale can live out of the water for up to two days. Refloating may only take a couple minutes. Rescuers then have a chance to wait for high tide and more helpers to arrive.

Whale rescuers also take measurements and blood samples of each whale. This data helps scientists learn more about why whales strand.

Returning whales to the ocean can take as long as four months.

Some whales have a greater chance for survival if they are taken to an animal care facility. Special boats are used if the whale can be taken to the facility by water. In other cases, trucks outfitted with slings and padding are used to carry the whales to their temporary home. After weeks of care, the whales may be able to be released to the ocean. Others may not be released because they would not survive in the wild. These whales remain in marine parks or aquariums.

The survival rate for stranded whales is very low. Many don't survive. By the time most stranded whales are discovered, it is too late to save them. Rescuers may need to make the difficult decision to let the whales die.

Groups devoted to stranded marine mammals are ready to help at all times. People who live in New Zealand see more than 300 whales and dolphins strand every year. Experts can recognize signs of stranding before it occurs. Groups of whales gathering near shore is a sign that they might strand. Boats or helicopters may be used to encourage the whales to swim back out to sea before the tides go out.

Whale researchers study samples taken from both living and dead whales. These samples help scientists answer the questions about whale strandings. The more people learn about why whales strand, the more they can do to prevent it.

Whale Strandings: Causes and Effects

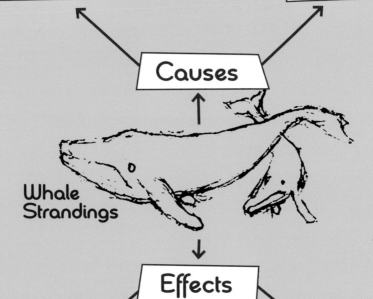

Physical

» confusion
» injury or illness
» starvation
» separation
» fear

Environmental

» global warming
» underwater noises
» military sonar
» low tides
» pollution

Causes

Whale Strandings

Effects

Immediate

» panic
» confusion
» stress
» overheating

Eventual

» crushed bodies
» muscle damage
» organ failure
» drowning
» death

Long term

» smaller whale
  population means
  less food for
  predators
» whale bodies can
  pollute beaches

RESOURCES TO HELP WHALES

AMERICAN CETACEAN SOCIETY

The oldest whale conservation group in the world, the American Cetacean Society hopes to spread the word about whales. The society's main goal is to provide easily accessable educational materials for anyone interested in protecting whales.

NATIONAL OCEANIC AND ATMOSPHERIC ADMINISTRATION (NOAA) OFFICE OF PROTECTED RESOURCES

The Office of Protected Resources provides information about conserving marine mammals. It is the office's belief that anyone, anywhere, can make a positive impact on marine life.

NATIONAL WILDLIFE FEDERATION

The National Wildlife Federation is the world's largest conservation organization. The group's goal is to protect wildlife and to restore natural habitats. They hope to educate people as a means to protect America's animals.

WHALE RELEASE AND STRANDING: NEWFOUNDLAND AND LABRADOR

A government-funded program, the Whale Release and Stranding Group helps fishermen rescue and release stranded whales. They train fishermen how to release whales on their own, and take samples of stranded whales for scientists.

Glossary

baleen (BAY-leen)—thin plates in the mouth of some whales; baleen whales use their baleen to trap food

cetacean (si-TAY-shuhn)—a member of the whale family

echolocation (eh-koh-loh-KAY-shuhn)—the process of using sounds and echoes to locate objects; whales use echolocation to find food

magnetic field (mag-NET-ic FEELD)—an area of moving electrical currents that affects other objects

navigate (NAV-uh-gate)—to decide the direction one should travel

parasite (PAIR-uh-site)—an animal or plant that needs to live on or inside another animal or plant to survive

sonar (SOH-nar)—a device that uses sound waves to find underwater objects; sonar stands for sound navigation and ranging

species (SPEE-sheez)—a group of animals with similar features; members of a species can mate and produce young

suffocate (SUHF-uh-kate)—to die from lack of oxygen

theory (THEE-ur-ee)—an idea that explains something that is unknown

Read More

Christopherson, Sara Cohen. *Top 50 Reasons to Care about Whales and Dolphins: Animals in Peril.* Top 50 Reasons to Care about Endangered Animals. Berkeley Heights, N.J.: Enslow Publishers, 2010.

Hodgkins, Fran. *The Whale Scientists: Solving the Mystery of Whale Strandings.* Scientists in the Field. Boston: Houghton Mifflin Co., 2007.

Nicklin, Flip, and Linda Nicklin. *Face to Face With Whales.* Face to Face With Animals. Washington, D.C.: National Geographic, 2008.

Internet Sites

FactHound offers a safe, fun way to find Internet sites related to this book. All of the sites on FactHound have been researched by our staff.

Here's all you do:

Visit *www.facthound.com*

FactHound will fetch the best sites for you!

Index